LIVING IN
THE BOOK ...
RUTH

Pearl

WESTBOW
PRESS®
A DIVISION OF THOMAS NELSON
& ZONDERVAN

Scripture taken from the King James Version of the Bible.

WestBow Press books may be ordered through booksellers or by contacting:

WestBow Press
A Division of Thomas Nelson & Zondervan
1663 Liberty Drive
Bloomington, IN 47403
www.westbowpress.com
1 (866) 928-1240

ISBN: 978-1-4908-9355-6 (sc)
ISBN: 978-1-4908-9354-9 (e)

Library of Congress Control Number: 2015911037

Print information available on the last page.

WestBow Press rev. date: 07/30/2015

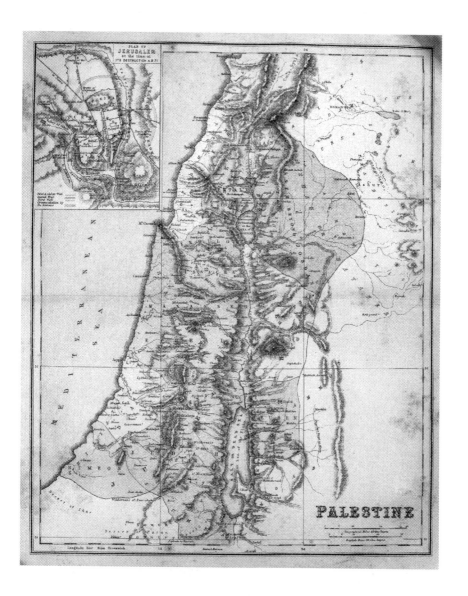

Living in the Book of the Bible Study Series: Ruth

This study will try to give examples of how people remain strong in character and true to God, even when the society around them is trying to collapse.

Key people: Ruth, Naomi, Boaz
Place: Moab, Bethlehem

Let's begin by reminding ourselves who the Moabites are (Genesis 19:30–38, Numbers 25).

We try to walk a fine line and not risk everything when we put our faith in Jesus Christ. God saves us, forgives us, rebuilds our lives, and gives us blessings that will last through eternity. Yet we hesitate again.

The godly man Boaz redeeming Ruth is a picture of how Jesus Christ redeems us. In the book of Ruth we find integrity, kindness, protections, prosperity blessing, faithfulness, and proof that even through our good and not-so-good decisions, our Father works in our lives to bring blessings to each person.

Even those who may not be walking with God at the present, He uses them for good and for the future of their lives and others' lives.

The book of Ruth is set in the times of Judges (Judges 2:16–18). The time is 1375–1250 BC. Matthew 1:5 shows that Boaz is in the lineage of Christ

Ruth 1 King James Version (KJV)

1 Now it came to pass in the days when the judges ruled, that there was a famine in the land. And a certain man of Bethlehem judah went to sojourn in the country of Moab, he, and his wife, and his two sons.

² And the name of the man was Elimelech, and the name of his wife Naomi, and the name of his two sons Mahlon and Chilion, Ephrathites of Bethlehem judah. And they came into the country of Moab, and continued there.

³ And Elimelech Naomi's husband died; and she was left, and her two sons.

⁴ And they took them wives of the women of Moab; the name of the one was Orpah, and the name of the other Ruth: and they dwelled there about ten years.

⁵ And Mahlon and Chilion died also both of them; and the woman was left of her two sons and her husband.

⁶ Then she arose with her daughters in law, that she might return from the country of Moab: for she had heard in the country of Moab how that the Lord had visited his people in giving them bread.

⁷ Wherefore she went forth out of the place where she was, and her two daughters in law with her; and they went on the way to return unto the land of Judah.

⁸And Naomi said unto her two daughters in law, Go, return each to her mother's house: the LORD deal kindly with you, as ye have dealt with the dead, and with me.

⁹The LORD grant you that ye may find rest, each of you in the house of her husband. Then she kissed them; and they lifted up their voice, and wept.

¹⁰And they said unto her, Surely we will return with thee unto thy people.

¹¹And Naomi said, Turn again, my daughters: why will ye go with me? are there yet any more sons in my womb, that they may be your husbands?

¹²Turn again, my daughters, go your way; for I am too old to have a husband. If I should say, I have hope, if I should have a husband also to night, and should also bear sons;

¹³Would ye tarry for them till they were grown? would ye stay for them from having husbands? nay, my daughters; for it grieveth me much for your sakes that the hand of the LORD is gone out against me.

¹⁴And they lifted up their voice, and wept again: and Orpah kissed her mother in law; but Ruth clave unto her.

¹⁵And she said, Behold, thy sister in law is gone back unto her people, and unto her gods: return thou after thy sister in law.

¹⁶And Ruth said, In treat me not to leave thee, or to return from following after thee: for whither thou goest, I will go; and where thou

lodgest, I will lodge: thy people shall be my people, and thy God my God:

[17] Where thou diest, will I die, and there will I be buried: the LORD do so to me, and more also, if ought but death part thee and me.

[18] When she saw that she was stedfastly minded to go with her, then she left speaking unto her.

[19] So they two went until they came to Bethlehem. And it came to pass, when they were come to Bethlehem, that all the city was moved about them, and they said, Is this Naomi?

[20] And she said unto them, Call me not Naomi, call me Mara: for the Almighty hath dealt very bitterly with me.

[21] I went out full and the LORD hath brought me home again empty: why then call ye me Naomi, seeing the LORD hath testified against me, and the Almighty hath afflicted me?

[22] So Naomi returned, and Ruth the Moabitess, her daughter in law, with her, which returned out of the country of Moab: and they came to Bethlehem in the beginning of barley harvest.

Ruth 2 King James Version (KJV)

2 And Naomi had a kinsman of her husband's, a mighty man of wealth, of the family of Elimelech; and his name was Boaz.

[2] And Ruth the Moabitess said unto Naomi, Let me now go to the field, and glean ears of corn after him in whose sight I shall find grace. And she said unto her, Go, my daughter.

[3] And she went, and came, and gleaned in the field after the reapers: and her hap was to light on a part of the field belonging unto Boaz, who was of the kindred of Elimelech.

[4] And, behold, Boaz came from Bethlehem, and said unto the reapers, The Lord be with you. And they answered him, The Lord bless thee.

[5] Then said Boaz unto his servant that was set over the reapers, Whose damsel is this?

[6] And the servant that was set over the reapers answered and said, It is the Moabitish damsel that came back with Naomi out of the country of Moab:

[7] And she said, I pray you, let me glean and gather after the reapers among the sheaves: so she came, and hath continued even from the morning until now, that she tarried a little in the house.

[8] Then said Boaz unto Ruth, Hearest thou not, my daughter? Go not to glean in another field, neither go from hence, but abide here fast by my maidens:

⁹ Let thine eyes be on the field that they do reap, and go thou after them: have I not charged the young men that they shall not touch thee? and when thou art athirst, go unto the vessels, and drink of that which the young men have drawn.

¹⁰ Then she fell on her face, and bowed herself to the ground, and said unto him, Why have I found grace in thine eyes, that thou shouldest take knowledge of me, seeing I am a stranger?

¹¹ And Boaz answered and said unto her, It hath fully been shewed me, all that thou hast done unto thy mother in law since the death of thine husband: and how thou hast left thy father and thy mother, and the land of thy nativity, and art come unto a people which thou knewest not heretofore.

¹² The LORD recompense thy work, and a full reward be given thee of the LORD God of Israel, under whose wings thou art come to trust.

¹³ Then she said, Let me find favour in thy sight, my lord; for that thou hast comforted me, and for that thou hast spoken friendly unto thine handmaid, though I be not like unto one of thine handmaidens.

¹⁴ And Boaz said unto her, At mealtime come thou hither, and eat of the bread, and dip thy morsel in the vinegar. And she sat beside the reapers: and he reached her parched corn, and she did eat, and was sufficed, and left.

¹⁵ And when she was risen up to glean, Boaz commanded his young men, saying, Let her glean even among the sheaves, and reproach her not:

¹⁶ And let fall also some of the handfuls of purpose for her, and leave them, that she may glean them, and rebuke her not.

[17] So she gleaned in the field until even, and beat out that she had gleaned: and it was about an ephah of barley.

[18] And she took it up, and went into the city: and her mother in law saw what she had gleaned: and she brought forth, and gave to her that she had reserved after she was sufficed.

[19] And her mother in law said unto her, Where hast thou gleaned to day? and where wroughtest thou? blessed be he that did take knowledge of thee. And she shewed her mother in law with whom she had wrought, and said, The man's name with whom I wrought to day is Boaz.

[20] And Naomi said unto her daughter in law, Blessed be he of the LORD, who hath not left off his kindness to the living and to the dead. And Naomi said unto her, The man is near of kin unto us, one of our next kinsmen.

[21] And Ruth the Moabitess said, He said unto me also, Thou shalt keep fast by my young men, until they have ended all my harvest.

[22] And Naomi said unto Ruth her daughter in law, It is good, my daughter, that thou go out with his maidens, that they meet thee not in any other field.

[23] So she kept fast by the maidens of Boaz to glean unto the end of barley harvest and of wheat harvest; and dwelt with her mother in law.

Ruth 3 King James Version (KJV)

3 Then Naomi her mother in law said unto her, My daughter, shall I not seek rest for thee, that it may be well with thee?

² And now is not Boaz of our kindred, with whose maidens thou wast? Behold, he winnows barley to night in the threshingfloor.

³ Wash thyself therefore, and anoint thee, and put thy raiment upon thee, and get thee down to the floor: but make not thyself known unto the man, until he shall have done eating and drinking.

⁴ And it shall be, when he lieth down, that thou shalt mark the place where he shall lie, and thou shalt go in, and uncover his feet, and lay thee down; and he will tell thee what thou shalt do.

⁵ And she said unto her, All that thou sayest unto me I will do.

⁶ And she went down unto the floor, and did according to all that her mother in law bade her.

⁷ And when Boaz had eaten and drunk, and his heart was merry, he went to lie down at the end of the heap of corn: and she came softly, and uncovered his feet, and laid her down.

⁸ And it came to pass at midnight, that the man was afraid, and turned himself: and, behold, a woman lay at his feet.

⁹ And he said, Who art thou? And she answered, I am Ruth thine handmaid: spread therefore thy skirt over thine handmaid; for thou art a near kinsman.

¹⁰ And he said, Blessed be thou of the LORD, my daughter: for thou hast shewed more kindness in the latter end than at the beginning, inasmuch as thou followedst not young men, whether poor or rich.

¹¹ And now, my daughter, fear not; I will do to thee all that thou request: for all the city of my people doth know that thou art a virtuous woman.

¹² And now it is true that I am thy near kinsman: howbeit there is a kinsman nearer than I.

¹³ Tarry this night, and it shall be in the morning, that if he will perform unto thee the part of a kinsman, well; let him do the kinsman's part: but if he will not do the part of a kinsman to thee, then will I do the part of a kinsman to thee, as the LORD liveth: lie down until the morning.

¹⁴ And she lay at his feet until the morning: and she rose up before one could know another. And he said, Let it not be known that a woman came into the floor.

¹⁵ Also he said, Bring the vail that thou hast upon thee, and hold it. And when she held it, he measured six measures of barley, and laid it on her: and she went into the city.

¹⁶ And when she came to her mother in law, she said, Who art thou, my daughter? And she told her all that the man had done to her.

¹⁷ And she said, These six measures of barley gave he me; for he said to me, Go not empty unto thy mother in law.

[18] Then said she, Sit still, my daughter, until thou know how the matter will fall: for the man will not be in rest, until he have finished the thing this day.

Ruth 4 King James Version (KJV)

4 Then went Boaz up to the gate, and sat him down there: and, behold, the kinsman of whom Boaz spake came by; unto whom he said, Ho, such a one! turn aside, sit down here. And he turned aside, and sat down.

² And he took ten men of the elders of the city, and said, Sit ye down here. And they sat down.

³ And he said unto the kinsman, Naomi, that is come again out of the country of Moab, selleth a parcel of land, which was our brother Elimelech's:

⁴ And I thought to advertise thee, saying, Buy it before the inhabitants, and before the elders of my people. If thou wilt redeem it, redeem it: but if thou wilt not redeem it, then tell me, that I may know: for there is none to redeem it beside thee; and I am after thee. And he said, I will redeem it.

⁵ Then said Boaz, What day thou buyest the field of the hand of Naomi, thou must buy it also of Ruth the Moabitess, the wife of the dead, to raise up the name of the dead upon his inheritance.

⁶ And the kinsman said, I cannot redeem it for myself, lest I mar mine own inheritance: redeem thou my right to thyself; for I cannot redeem it.

⁷ Now this was the manner in former time in Israel concerning redeeming and concerning changing, for to confirm all things; a man plucked off his shoe, and gave it to his neighbour: and this was a testimony in Israel.

⁸ Therefore the kinsman said unto Boaz, Buy it for thee. So he drew off his shoe.

⁹ And Boaz said unto the elders, and unto all the people, Ye are witnesses this day, that I have bought all that was Elimelech's, and all that was Chilion's and Mahlon's, of the hand of Naomi.

¹⁰ Moreover Ruth the Moabitess, the wife of Mahlon, have I purchased to be my wife, to raise up the name of the dead upon his inheritance, that the name of the dead be not cut off from among his brethren, and from the gate of his place: ye are witnesses this day.

¹¹ And all the people that were in the gate, and the elders, said, We are witnesses. The LORD make the woman that is come into thine house like Rachel and like Leah, which two did build the house of Israel: and do thou worthily in Ephratah, and be famous in Bethlehem:

¹² And let thy house be like the house of Pharez, whom Tamar bare unto Judah, of the seed which the LORD shall give thee of this young woman.

¹³ So Boaz took Ruth, and she was his wife: and when he went in unto her, the LORD gave her conception, and she bare a son.

¹⁴ And the women said unto Naomi, Blessed be the LORD, which hath not left thee this day without a kinsman, that his name may be famous in Israel.

[15] And he shall be unto thee a restorer of thy life, and a nourisher of thine old age: for thy daughter in law, which loveth thee, which is better to thee than seven sons, hath born him.

[16] And Naomi took the child, and laid it in her bosom, and became nurse unto it.

[17] And the women her neighbours gave it a name, saying, There is a son born to Naomi; and they called his name Obed: he is the father of Jesse, the father of David.

[18] Now these are the generations of Pharez: Pharez begat Hezron,

[19] And Hezron begat Ram, and Ram begat Amminadab,

[20] And Amminadab begat Nahshon, and Nahshon begat Salmon,

[21] And Salmon begat Boaz, and Boaz begat Obed,

[22] And Obed begat Jesse, and Jesse begat David.

As we read about the lives of these individuals in their own times, we have to acknowledge they had harder lives than we do today. At the same time, the famine they experienced was different from what we deal with today. Or was it? A famine of spirit is just as bad as a famine of food.

There are times in working your way through this series of studies when you will see a *kiss from God*. I call these moments *kisses from God* because there are times when only the Spirit of God could have given me the notion I am sharing with you. I say *God blew me a kiss* of acknowledgment, proving that He chooses His instruments to fulfill His plans.

Brief Overview of the Book of Ruth

- Naomi was the wife of Elimelech and mother of two sons, Mahlon and Chilion.
- Elimelech, her husband, died, and the sons brought Naomi into their home and took care of her for approximately ten years.
- The Bible shares examples that demonstrate that life goes on after a family member dies.
- Elimelech must have died when he was very young because life went on for about ten years after his death.
- There was a famine prior to Elimelech's death, and he moved the family from Bethlehem to Moab.

This all sounds very normal up to this point, doesn't it? The father moved the family for a job, and then they moved back to be closer to other relatives. The kids brought their parents home. Input your situation or circumstance here.

REVIEW OF CHAPTER 1

Both sons, Mahlon and Chilion, married Moabite women. This did not please their mama. In the Old Testament, Moabites were discriminated against.

> an Ammonite or a Moabite shall not enter the assembly of the LORD; even to the 10th generation none of his descendants shall enter the assembly of the LORD forever, because they did not meet you with bread and water on the road when you came out of Egypt and because they hired against you Balaam the son of Beor for Pethor of Mesopotamia to curse you. Never the less the LORD YOUR God would not list to Balaam, but the LORD your God turned the curse into blessing for you because the LORD your God loves you. You shall not seek their peace nor their prosperity all your days forever. (Deuteronomy 23:3–6)

Even so, the Moabites were tolerated as they lived outside the Promised Land. Moabites were not allowed to worship at the tabernacle because they had not let the Israelites pass through the land during the Exodus from Egypt.

Now we have to remember this passage is set during the time of the Old Testament. God's timing is exact and all knowing; we may not understand all of His rules and regulations, but when God was making the nation, His plan overrode humanity's control. God hates sin but loves the sinner. But here is what I love: God is about to change the players and show that He works through Gentiles, in the early stages, to show courage and moral living.

Isn't that what we're trying to do today? We want to have the courage to live morally and to have biblical standards in our lives. I know I deal with that daily.

I want to _____

But I should _____

I choose to _____

So we pick up ten years later, with the characters stuck in the middle of their lives. Mahlon had a wife named Orpah, and Chilion had Ruth as his wife. (We assume Mahlon was the older because this is the order they are listed in the Bible.) The book states the following:

> Now they took wives of the women of Moab: the name
> of the one [was] Orpah, and the name of the other Ruth.
> And they dwelt there about ten years. (Ruth 1:4–5)

Then both Mahlon and Chilion died, so Naomi survived her two sons and her husband. All of her days seemed to be part of living a normal life:

- She got up in the morning, prayed, and had devotions. (There is an argument at this point that some went to the synagogue before breakfast and prayed while some went after. Whatever the time frame, they went before working or performing daily chores.)
- She worked and performed her daily routine.
- She went to synagogue for lessons and prayers.
- She had dinner, cleaned up, and had fellowship with family.

- She planned tomorrow's schedule.
- She prayed and went to sleep.

They all participated in daily life, so they could enjoy each other during the day, praise and thank God for each blessing, and then allow the body to rest to begin again the next day. Sounds like a perfect day to me.

Kiss from God: God has plans—God puts His plans into action.

Mahlon and Chilion died, leaving their wives as widows and their mother, who was already a widow. This meant the family had three widows in a time of famine. In this time, being a widow was like being jobless and homeless today. They were taken advantage of and ignored and lived in poverty in a bad area of town.

God's law provided for them to go to the nearest relative of the dead husband to care for them. There was no family where they lived, however; remember that Elimelech had moved his young family from Bethlehem because of the famine. So for Naomi, there was no one. Naomi did what she thought was her only choice; she went back to the land of her people and hoped there were still relatives alive who would take care of her. Naomi, being what we would call a realist, told her daughters-in-law to go back to their families; she released them from any obligation they may have felt. Naomi had a selfless attitude. She had made her decision to go back to her land of Judah and live out her last days there.

Naomi encouraged Orpah and Ruth to say in Moab and be with their families. "Find a new love," she said, in essence, "have children, and live out your days as God intends." Do you have any doubt that this was God's plan? Neither son had children; daily life went on for over ten years. She kissed them, and they each wept and held onto one another. The daughters cried out, "No, we will go with you!"

> If brothers dwell together, and one of them dies and has no son, the widow of the dead man shall not be [married] to a stranger outside [the family]; her husband's brother shall go in to her, take her as his wife, and perform the duty of a husband's brother to her. And it shall be [that] the firstborn son which she bears will succeed to the name of his dead brother, that his name may not be blotted out of Israel. But if the man does not want to take his brother's wife, then let his brother's wife go up to the gate to the elders, and say, *"My husband's brother refuses to raise up a name to his brother in Israel; he will not perform the duty of my husband's brother." Then the elders of his city shall call him and speak to him. But [if] he stands firm and says, "I do not want to take her," then his brother's wife shall come to him in the presence of the elders, remove his sandal from his foot, spit in his face, and answer and say, "So shall it be done to the man who will not build up his brother's house." And his name shall be called in Israel, "The house of him who had his sandal removed.* (Deuteronomy 25:5–10)

Naomi, again acting selflessly, asked why they would come with her. They had no husbands, so there would be no children. Even if Naomi did have more sons, it would be years before they would be born, and Orpah and Ruth would soon be past childbearing age. She said, "Do not restrain yourself from life, having husbands, having children … as much as it grieves me for your sake, remain in our homeland and remarry, continue on."

In Ruth 1:14, Orpah agreed, and again they lifted up their voices and wept. Orpah kissed her mother-in-law, but Ruth clung to Naomi. Ruth was willing to give up the possibility of security and children to care for Naomi. There is a lot we don't know here. We don't know if Ruth had a family; we assume she did because Naomi said, "Go to your family."

We don't know if Naomi was more of a mother to Ruth than her biological mother; we don't know if Ruth's family was stern in their rules and said, "Don't come back." There were harsh realities then, just as there are now. What we do know is God's hand said, "Go with Naomi." So Ruth clung to her mother-in-law. Even though Ruth was a Moabite who worshiped many gods, she worshiped the one true God for at least ten years that we know of. This did not stop God from accepting her worship, which was pleasing to Ruth.

Jews are not the only people God loves, either back then or today. Jews were the people He chose to show how the rest of the world would come to know Him. Christ was born a Jew for this reason; through Jesus Christ the entire world eventually will know God. As Acts 10:35 reminds us, "But in every nation whoever fears Him and works righteousness is accepted by Him." Ruth was blessed for her faithfulness, not because of her race. As it turned out, Ruth was the great-grandmother of King David, a direct ancestor of Jesus. No one is ever disqualified to serve God, not because of race, sex, national background—nothing. God used every circumstance to build His kingdom.

Ruth pleaded with Naomi, asking Naomi not to make her leave. Ruth wanted to go with her, to live wherever she lived, to call Naomi's kin her family, Naomi's God her God, so that nothing short of death would separate them. This verse or statement tells us a lot about Ruth. Remember that the Moabites worshiped many gods, but Ruth had just committed herself to worshiping the one true God. She could not go back to her family with this knowledge and religion. Her family would not accept her, and she probably could not live that way again.

Naomi saw in Ruth 1:18 that the "girl" was not going to listen to her, so Naomi "stopped speaking to her." As women of faith, we can interpret this passage as follows:

- It could mean she stopped and didn't argue with her any longer.
- It could mean that by not speaking to her, Ruth hoped she would change her mind.
- It could mean that she was pouting and torturing Ruth for not doing what Naomi told her to do. Naomi had not knowledge if she even had family left in Bethlehem … Would they accept Naomi, let alone another widow? But we know God would bless them both.

Two women traveling together is not all that uncommon nowadays, but back then, it was very dangerous and uncommon. As nowadays, there were thieves (carjackers), pirates, wild animals, or even weather problems. We have to know God guided them because the next thing we know, they were entering Bethlehem.

Naomi must have been well known because verse 19 says, "All the city was excited to see them. Naomi is it you?" Here we see a different side of Naomi. She was home, yet she seemed to harbor some ill feelings. In verse 20 she said, "Don't call me Naomi, call me Mara (literally means bitter)." Wasn't she where she wanted to be?

Can you relate? I can. She left with her husband because of the famine. They needed to make a better life for their family; now she was coming back without a husband, without her children, a widow, with nothing but bitterness, feeling God had left her. But we see God was all around her. Why then do we not see Him at our every need?

Naomi was back home, in Bethlehem, with her daughter-in-law, Ruth the Moabitess. They came to Bethlehem at the beginning of barley harvest. (This is also from the hand of God.) The barley harvest takes place in the spring, which is also a time of hope and plenty. Bethlehem was a farming community at the time, and since it was harvest time, there was plenty of leftover grain in the field. This leftover grain could be collected (gleaned) and made into food.

Leviticus 19:9 says, "When you reap the harvest of your land, you shall not wholly reap the corners of your field, nor shall you gather the gleanings of your harvest."

Leviticus 23:22 says, "When you reap the harvest of your land, you shall not wholly reap the corners of your field when you reap, nor shall you gather any gleaning from your harvest. You shall leave them for the poor and for the stranger: I [am] the LORD your God."

Deuteronomy 24:19 says, "When you reap your harvest in your field, and forget a sheaf in the field, you shall not go back to get it; it shall be for the stranger, the fatherless, and the widow, that the LORD your God may bless you in all the work of your hands."

These laws dictate how the fields are harvested. This allowed the poor to eat and prevented owners from hoarding.

REVIEW OF CHAPTER 2

Do you see this law as God's hand to help out the poor or a working welfare plan in Israel?

Maybe we should be counting how many fingers God has.

Naomi's in-laws just happened to have land and wealth. One of the relatives' names was Boaz. Ruth asked Naomi to let her go into the family field and collect grain. Ruth was willing and able to go into the field and gather what was needed. God allowed Ruth to provide for them both. If you are waiting for God to provide, consider that He may be waiting for you to take a step so He can be next to you each step of the way.

Naomi sent her, saying, "Go, daughter." (Notice the "in-law" was gone this time.) Ruth went and collected grain in the field after the laborers. As she followed the laborers, they told her they were going to enter another field, belonging to a relative (Boaz).

Boaz asked his workers who this woman was. The workers told Boaz she was the Moabite who came with his relative, Naomi.

Boaz was a gentleman. He went to Ruth and said, "Listen to me. Only follow my laborers. They've been commanded not to touch you. For a drink of water, only drink what my young men have drawn."

Ruth showed her appreciation to Boaz by verse 10 by "falling on her face, bowed down on the ground. 'Why have I found favor in your eyes, that you even notice me, since I am a foreigner?'" Ruth saw herself as foreigner, but Boaz saw her taking care of her mother-in-law. She left her family to make sure she was taken care of and came to a land she did not know.

Had she considered herself too proud for or too embarrassed to go into the field, she would not have met Boaz. It would have been an opportunity missed and a total change in her life. She became the ancestor of a king and the Messiah. But then we knew that, didn't we? God's hands were there the whole time. He gave Ruth the strength, allowing her the blessings of caring for Naomi. Ruth had the faith, and God supplied the rest.

Ruth exhibited admirable qualities. She was a hard worker, loving and kind, and faithful and brave. These qualities gained her a good reputation, but only because Ruth displayed them consistently. Her words matched her actions. No matter where she was, what she said, her character remained the same.

What about you? Can you, or people around you, say that about you? Do you know what your character is? Do you know what your reputation is? These are formed by the people around you at work, in town, at home, at church, wherever you go.

This comes by living out the qualities you believe in consistently, no matter what group of people or surroundings you find yourself in.

Boaz offered Ruth food at meal time with him and his workers. In the time we are studying, Boaz was offering her a relationship. Just as we share meals with friends and fellowship, Boaz was building relationships with the workers and offered her the same. She accepted.

After finishing the meal, they all went back to work.

> ➢ Boaz instructed his laborers to allow her to collect wherever she wanted.
> ➢ They were to drop grain purposely for her to collect. Ruth collected grain all evening.
> ➢ She processed it and took it back to Naomi.

Ruth brought the processed grain home, and the two ladies talked as the product was being taken care of. (Can you hear them discussing the happenings of the day? "This happened, then he said. I said ...") Ruth said the man that allowed her to collect the grain was Boaz.

Naomi said, "Blessed are we. He is a relation of ours, one of our close relatives." Ruth continued to tell her mother (in-law) that Boaz told her she could continue to get grain as long as she stayed close to the laborers until they were done, which Ruth did. Naomi may have felt better at first to come home, but her faith in God was still alive. She praised God for Boaz's kindness to Ruth. Naomi trusted God and acknowledged His goodness.

Each day is a new opportunity for experiencing God's care. We see most of the fingers God has in Naomi and Ruth's lives, but He is in our lives also. Look for Him.

In God's plan nothing "just happen," and there are no "coincidences." Nothing ends up any other way but God's way. Never close the door on what God is able to do. There is no luck or coincidence. Have faith that God is directing our lives for His kingdom.

REVIEW OF CHAPTER 3

Here comes the sticky part. We have to know some cultural details to understand what Naomi asked Ruth to do. The future for both women at the time was bleak to say the least; as we discussed earlier, they were both widows.

We see Naomi trying to match make her daughter (in-law) with Boaz. See, mamas three thousand years ago were no different than today! Naomi didn't ask Ruth to do anything bad, against the law, or immoral, but maybe she used Satan's society and gossip for God's benefit.

Boaz was a relative of Naomi's dead husband, which means he was a kinsman redeemer. A kinsman redeemer is a relative who volunteers to take responsibility for the extended family. Earlier we looked up and discussed Deuteronomy 25:5–10. (Review if you need).

Do you get that the Jews not only knew the Scripture but lived by it? Scripture was, and is, the rules for life. Tough choices were not about self, but "How do I get back into good graces and correct living with God?" and so the Sadducees did it also.

Be good, do good, others see the good. Could you do it? They always had to be on guard to follow all the laws. They had to know them all to follow and then make it look good all the time … I'm out! Probably before I even got started.

This law allows a widow to marry a relative or brother. But Naomi had no sons left, so this defaulted to the next closest relative. Oh yeah, there are rules here too. The closest did not have to accept the "chore." It then moved down the line until one said yes or there were no more relatives. If there were no relatives willing, the widow (in this case widows) would live in poverty—homeless. We will not go there, because God doesn't allow it this time.

Our kinsman-redeemer is Christ. He was God. He came to earth as man, flesh and blood, to save us. His death on the cross redeemed us from sin and hopelessness, purchasing each of us to be His own possession.

> Knowing that you were not redeemed with corruptible things, [like] silver or gold, from your aimless conduct [received] by tradition from your fathers, but with the precious blood of Christ, as of a lamb without blemish and without spot. (1 Peter 1:18–19)

Jesus Christ guaranteed each of us eternal inheritance. *Ahhhh,* feel the peace ... But that hasn't happened yet. We are seeing how the ancestors lived. Naomi reiterated that Boaz was a relative, so she put a plan into action. Now I say "a plan," not "her plan," because I believe Naomi was just doing (saying) what God told her.

Naomi seemed to know Boaz would be "winnowing" or processing the harvest that night. Therefore Naomi said in verses 3 and 4, "Wash yourself and anoint yourself, put on your best garment, go down to the threshing floor, do not make yourself known to the man until he has finished eating and drinking (his evening meal). Then it shall be, when he lies down, that you shall notice the place where he lies; you will go in, uncover his fee, and lie down' and he will tell you what to do." How many fingers does God have in this one?

"Therefore wash yourself and anoint yourself, put on your [best] garment and go down to the threshing floor; [but] do not make yourself known to the man until he has finished eating and drinking. Then it shall be, when he lies down, that you shall notice the place where he lies; and you shall go in, uncover his feet, and lie down; and he will tell you what you should do." Ruth says, "All that you say to me I will do." So she went down to the threshing floor and did according to all that her mother-in-law instructed her. She follows instruction the exact timing. (Ruth 3:3–6)

➢ **Kiss from God:** God's timing is perfect. Around midnight Boaz was startled.

➢ **Kiss from God:** God woke him up. Can you hear God saying, "Look at your future"?

➢ **Kiss from God:** Boaz was startled. He found a woman lying at his feet. In verse 9 he asked, "Who are you?" She replied, "I am Ruth your maidservant. Take your maidservant under your wing, for you are a close relative."

➢ **Kiss from God:** Ruth put herself out on a limb. She trusted Naomi and knew she only had Ruth's future in mind. But she didn't know Boaz, did she? Ruth met him in the field, with the laborers. He gave her food and protected her from other laborers. But this was pure faith. Can you hear all the what-ifs from small or non-believers? Ruth didn't. God guided her right in that barn and sat her down next to Boaz.

In verse 10 Boaz told her how kind and virtuous she was. Actually Proverbs 31:1–31 (complete verses at end of chapter) says it the same way. In verse 11 Boaz said, "I will do for you all you request, for all the people know what kind of person you are; faithful, kind, you have integrity, are protective of your mother-in-law." Do you hear the but in verse 12: "However, there is one relative closer than I."

➤ **Kiss from God:** Do you get the impression he's thought about this and looked into the situation already? He knew there was one closer who had the option of taking Ruth.

However, Boaz, being the man of God, said in verse 13, "Stay the night. In the morning if he does not do the duty—good, I will do the right duty." Can you feel his heart beating, the comfort in his voice, the praying in his mind? He was anxious for the blessing. "Lord, I have been single so long. This is the wife I have prayed for …"

Verse 14 says, "So she lay at his feet until morning, and she arose before one could recognize another." Boaz didn't want Ruth's character or integrity tarnished, so he told his laborers, "You saw nothing." Boaz filled Ruth's shawl with barley, and she went into the city.

As Ruth went into the home, Naomi said, "Is that you, my daughter?" Oh my goodness can you hear the eagerness for information in her voice? See the eyelashes flutter? Can you see the overwhelming smile, the open arms waiting to hug her? God can do a romance, can't He!

Ruth told her exactly what happened and how Boaz said, "Do not go empty-handed to your mother-in-law." Naomi told her daughter (in-law) to "rest until he has concluded the matter this day."

Let's take this part a little farther. We all know what happened on the threshing floor … nothing! But gossip will not allow anything to happen. God took the situation and finished it before anyone had a chance to get hold of it. This is a way that Satan persecutes Christians. We may be innocent, but that is boring. So a little white lie is added to an innocent act to alert everyone's attention. But when we trust in faith, in God, as Ruth did, it all works out.

Naomi knew Boaz's reputation and knew he would not rest until it was cleared up. (But it would be better than cleared up ... it would be God's plan carried out.)

Do you know reliable people like this? Can you look back at any situation and see God's hand guiding the resolution? Are you the one who does as you say?

Keep your word and follow through. This cannot be built all at once with a load of bricks. It must be built one brick at a time; it takes years.

REVIEW OF CHAPTER 4

Boaz went to see the closest (living) relative and explained about the law and all the stipulations (Leviticus 25:25). The relative said he could not redeem it for himself, so Boaz was clear to have the right to redemption. Of course he did. God made it so! Now, all us shoe people rejoice. Verse 7 explains the custom in former times in Israel concerning redeeming and exchanging to confirm anything; you took your sandal off and gave it to the other. This was confirmation in Israel.

All this did not take place in private. There had to be witnesses and people around. This all took place at the gate of the city of Bethlehem. The gate was the "city hall" of any city. Business and court took place at the gate. Travelers came and left here also.

In verse 8 the close relative said to Boaz, "Buy it for yourself." The relative took off his sandal. In verse 9 Boaz said to the elders and all the people, "You are witnesses this day ..." Verses 10 through 12 say the following:

> "Moreover, Ruth the Moabitess, the widow of Mahlon,
> I have acquired as my wife, to perpetuate the name of
> the dead through his inheritance, which the name of the
> dead may not be cut off from among his brethren and
> from his position at the gate. You are witnesses this day."
> And all the people who were at the gate, and the elders,
> said, "We are witnesses. The LORD make the woman
> who is coming to your house like Rachel and Leah, the
> two who built the house of Israel; and may you prosper
> in Ephrathah and be famous in Bethlehem. May your

house be like the house of Perez, whom Tamar bore to Judah, because of the offspring which the LORD will give you from this young woman."

Perez—where did Perez come from? Perez's birth was an example of levirate practice, where the brother or relative the dead husband married his widow (Genesis 38). Boaz was following levirate practice since Ruth's former husband had no living brothers. The descendants of Perez made Judah a prominent tribe. Boaz, David, and all the Judean kings were descendants of Perez. Verses 13 through 17 say the following:

> So Boaz took Ruth and she became his wife; and when he went in to her, the LORD gave her conception, and she bore a son. Then the women said to Naomi, "Blessed [be] the LORD, who has not left you this day without a close relative; and may his name be famous in Israel! And may he be to you a restorer of life and a nourisher of your old age; for your daughter-in-law, who loves you, who is better to you than seven sons, has borne him." Then Naomi took the child and laid him on her bosom, and became a nurse to him. Also the neighbor women gave him a name, saying, "There is a son born to Naomi." And they called his name Obed. He [is] the father of Jesse, the father of David.

Ruth's love for her mother (in-law) was known and recognized throughout Bethlehem. From the beginning we see kindness, even though there was tragedy and tough times, Naomi and Ruth trusted God. In God's time and abundant blessings, God always was there. When tragedy strikes, lean harder on God. Allow Him and trust Him. He is with you at all times.

Does this true Bible story show you the loving-kindness of God? Do you see each place where God touched their lives? Even though God's plan must be done, God cares for each of us, blesses each of us, and completes His plan. The births of David and Jesus Christ were accomplished through a loving, caring God.

We are unaware of God's bigger picture or the full purpose and importance of our lives. In our eternal lives when we look back, our perspective will be totally different. God must be part of each decision we make and keep His eternal values in mind. Ruth proved in her life that faithful obedience was significant, even though she was unaware of it at the time

Live knowing faithfulness to God is significant to your life and will extend beyond your lifetime. Here's proof the rewards (blessings) will outweigh any sacrifice you make. Verses 18 through 22 say the following:

> Now this [is] the genealogy of Perez: Perez begot Hezron;
> Hezron begot Ram, and Ram begot Amminadab;
> Amminadab begot Nahshon, and Nahshon begot
> Salmon; Salmon begot Boaz, and Boaz begot Obed;
> Obed begot Jesse, and Jesse begot David.

> The words of King Lemuel, the utterance which his
> mother taught him: What, my son? And what, son of
> my womb? And what, son of my vows? Do not give
> your strength to women, Nor your ways to that which
> destroys kings. [It is] not for kings, O Lemuel, [It is]
> not for kings to drink wine, Nor for princes intoxicating
> drink; Lest they drink and forget the law, And pervert
> the justice of all the afflicted. Give strong drink to him

who is perishing, And wine to those who are bitter of heart. Let him drink and forget his poverty, And remember his misery no more. Open your mouth for the speechless, In the cause of all [who are] appointed to die. Open your mouth, judge righteously, And plead the cause of the poor and needy. Who can find a virtuous wife? For her worth [is] far above rubies. The heart of her husband safely trusts her; So he will have no lack of gain. She does him good and not evil All the days of her life. She seeks wool and flax, And willingly works with her hands. She is like the merchant ships, She brings her food from afar. She also rises while it is yet night, And provides food for her household, And a portion for her maidservants. She considers a field and buys it; From her profits she plants a vineyard. She girds herself with strength, And strengthens her arms. She perceives that her merchandise [is] good, And her lamp does not go out by night. She stretches out her hands to the distaff, And her hand holds the spindle. She extends her hand to the poor, Yes, she reaches out her hands to the needy. She is not afraid of snow for her household, For all her household [is] clothed with scarlet. She makes tapestry for herself; Her clothing [is] fine linen and purple. Her husband is known in the gates, When he sits among the elders of the land. She makes linen garments and sells [them], And supplies sashes for the merchants. Strength and honor [are] her clothing; She shall rejoice in time to come. She opens her mouth with wisdom, And on her tongue [is] the law of kindness. She watches over the ways of her household, And does not eat the bread of idleness. Her children rise up and call her blessed; Her husband [also], and he praises her: "Many daughters have done well, But you excel them all." Charm [is] deceitful and beauty [is] passing, But a woman [who] fears the LORD, she shall be praised. Give her of the fruit of her hands, And let her own works praise her in the gates. (Proverbs 31:1–31)

Printed in the United States
By Bookmasters